Tracing Letters
Writing l

To parents
Write your child's name and the date in the boxes above.
When your child completes each exercise, praise him or her.

■ Read the words aloud.
Then say the sound of the letter as you trace it.

L

l

lion

lemon

| a | b | c | d | e | f | g | h | i | j | k | l | m | n | o | p | q | r | s | t | u | v | w | x | y | z |

■Read the words aloud.
  Then say the sound of the letter as you trace it.

lion

lemon

lion

lemon

leg

lamp

leg

lamp

Name

Date

■ Read the words aloud.
Then say the sound of the letter as you trace it.

T

t

tomato

tent

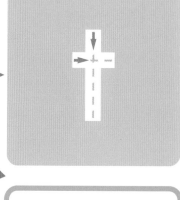

| a | b | c | d | e | f | g | h | i | j | k | l | m | n | o | p | q | r | s | t | u | v | w | x | y | z |

■ Read the words aloud.
Then say the sound of the letter as you trace it.

tomato

tomato

omato

tent

tent

ent

tennis

tennis

ennis

towel

towel

owel

Tracing Letters
Writing i

Name

Date

■ Read the words aloud.
Then say the sound of the letter as you trace it.

I

i

ink

ill

a b c d e f g h **i** j k l m n o p q r s t u v w x y z

■ Read the words aloud.
  Then say the sound of the letter as you trace it.

ink

ill

ink

ill

nk

ll

igloo

itch

igloo

itch

gloo

tch

Review
Writing l, t, and i

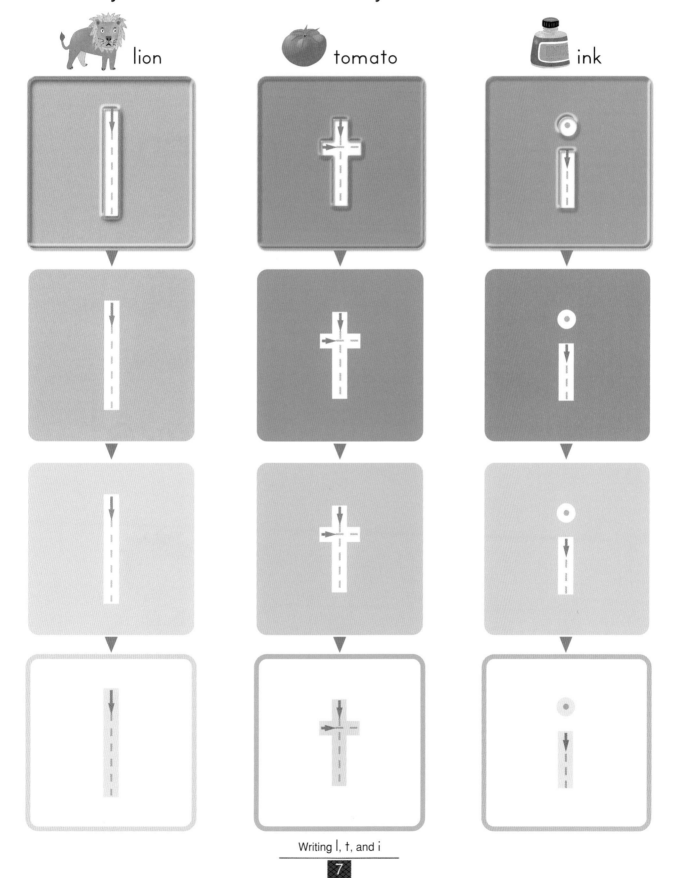

■ Read the words aloud.
  Then say the sound of the letter as you trace it.

lion   tomato   ink

■ Read the words aloud.
   Then say the sound of the letter as you trace it.

eg

amp

ennis

owel

gloo

tch

Tracing Letters
Writing j

Name

Date

■ Read the words aloud.
Then say the sound of the letter as you trace it.

J

j

jam

jet

| a | b | c | d | e | f | g | h | i | j | k | l | m | n | o | p | q | r | s | t | u | v | w | x | y | z |

■ Read the words aloud.
  Then say the sound of the letter as you trace it.

jam

jet

jam

jet

am

et

jump

jacket

jump

jacket

ump

acket

Name	
Date	

■ Read the words aloud.
 Then say the sound of the letter as you trace it.

F

f

fox

frog

| a | b | c | d | e | **f** | g | h | i | j | k | l | m | n | o | p | q | r | s | t | u | v | w | x | y | z |

■ Read the words aloud.
Then say the sound of the letter as you trace it.

fox

fox

ox

frog

frog

rog

fish

fish

ish

fence

fence

ence

Tracing Letters
Writing v

■ Read the words aloud.
   Then say the sound of the letter as you trace it.

van

valley

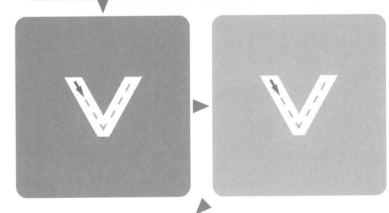

a	b	c	d	e	f	g	h	i	j	k	l	m	n	o	p	q	r	s	t	u	v	w	x	y	z

■ Read the words aloud.
  Then say the sound of the letter as you trace it.

van

valley

van

valley

van

valley

vest

vegetables

vest

vegetables

vest

vegetables

Review

Writing j, f, and v

Name

Date

■ Read the words aloud.
Then say the sound of the letter as you trace it.

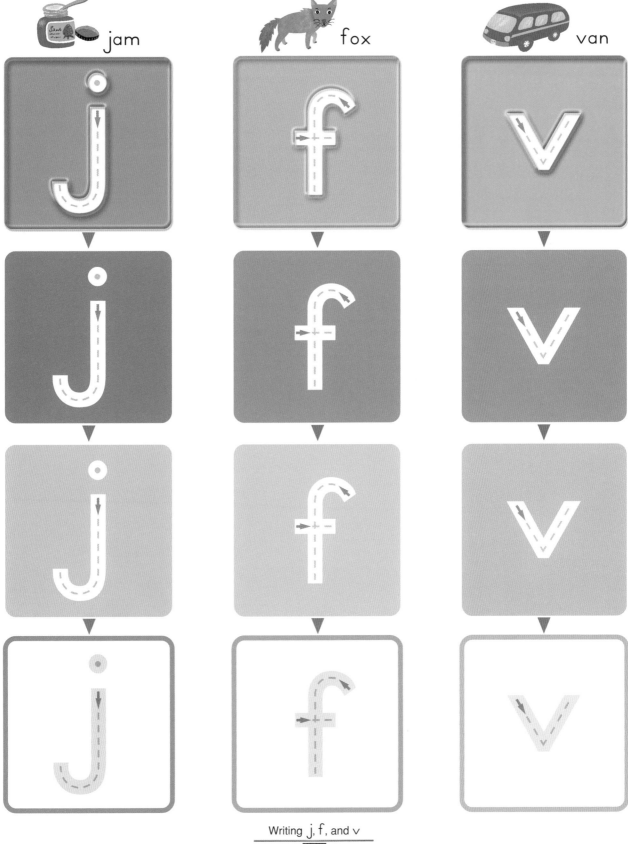

jam

fox

van

■ Read the words aloud.
   Then say the sound of the letter as you trace it.

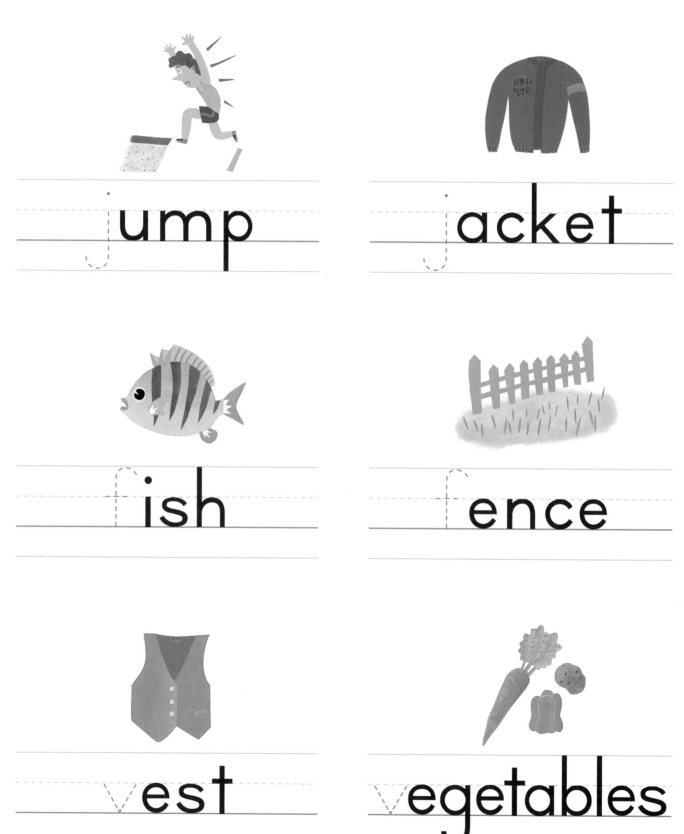

jump

jacket

fish

fence

vest

vegetables

Name

Date

■ Read the words aloud.
Then say the sound of the letter as you trace it.

W

w

water

wall

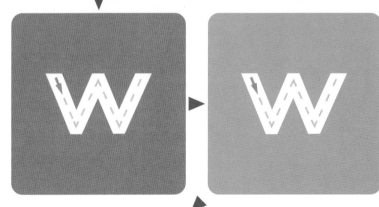

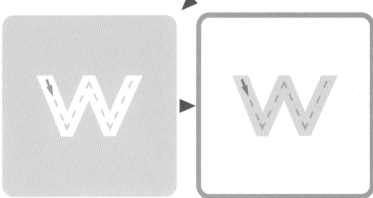

a b c d e f g h i j k l m n o p q r s t u v **w** x y z

■ Read the words aloud.
  Then say the sound of the letter as you trace it.

water

water

water

wall

wall

wall

wet

wet

wet

wash

wash

wash

Tracing Letters
Writing r

Name	
Date	

- Read the words aloud.
  Then say the sound of the letter as you trace it.

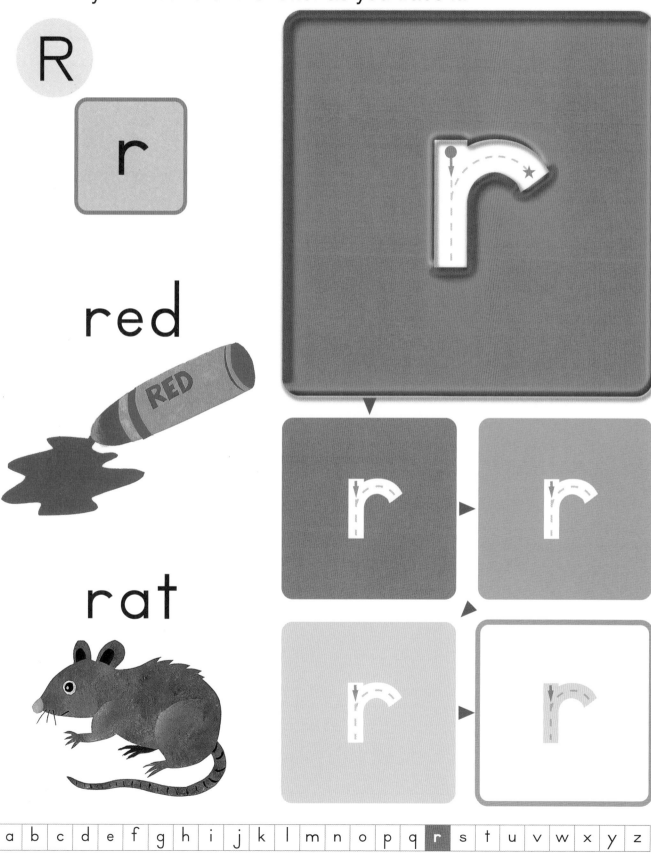

R

r

red

rat

a b c d e f g h i j k l m n o p q r s t u v w x y z

■ Read the words aloud.
 Then say the sound of the letter as you trace it.

red

red

red

rat

rat

rat

ring

ring

ring

run

run

run

Tracing Letters
Writing n

Name

Date

▪ Read the words aloud.
  Then say the sound of the letter as you trace it.

N

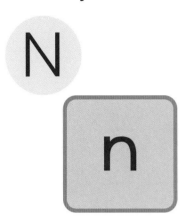

nut

net

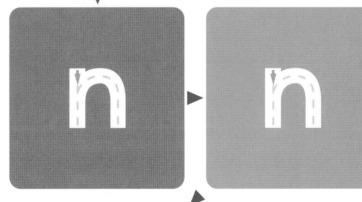

| a | b | c | d | e | f | g | h | i | j | k | l | m | **n** | o | p | q | r | s | t | u | v | w | x | y | z |

■ Read the words aloud.
   Then say the sound of the letter as you trace it.

nut

net

nut

net

nut

net

nest

needle

nest

needle

nest

needle

12 Review

Writing w, r, and n

■ Read the words aloud.
 Then say the sound of the letter as you trace it.

water red nut

w r n

w r n

w r n

w r n

■ Read the words aloud.
  Then say the sound of the letter as you trace it.

wet

wash

ring

run

nest

needle

Name

Date

■ Read the words aloud.
Then say the sound of the letter as you trace it.

H

h

hat

hen

| a | b | c | d | e | f | g | **h** | i | j | k | l | m | n | o | p | q | r | s | t | u | v | w | x | y | z |

■Read the words aloud.
  Then say the sound of the letter as you trace it.

hat

hen

hat

hen

hat

hen

hand

house

hand

house

hand

house

Tracing Letters
Writing m

■ Read the words aloud.
  Then say the sound of the letter as you trace it.

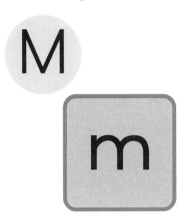

mat

map

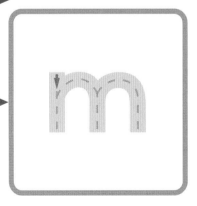

| a | b | c | d | e | f | g | h | i | j | k | l | **m** | n | o | p | q | r | s | t | u | v | w | x | y | z |

■ Read the words aloud.
  Then say the sound of the letter as you trace it.

mat

map

mat

map

mat

map

milk

moon

milk

moon

milk

moon

Tracing Letters
Writing x

■ Read the words aloud.
  Then say the sound of the letter as you trace it.

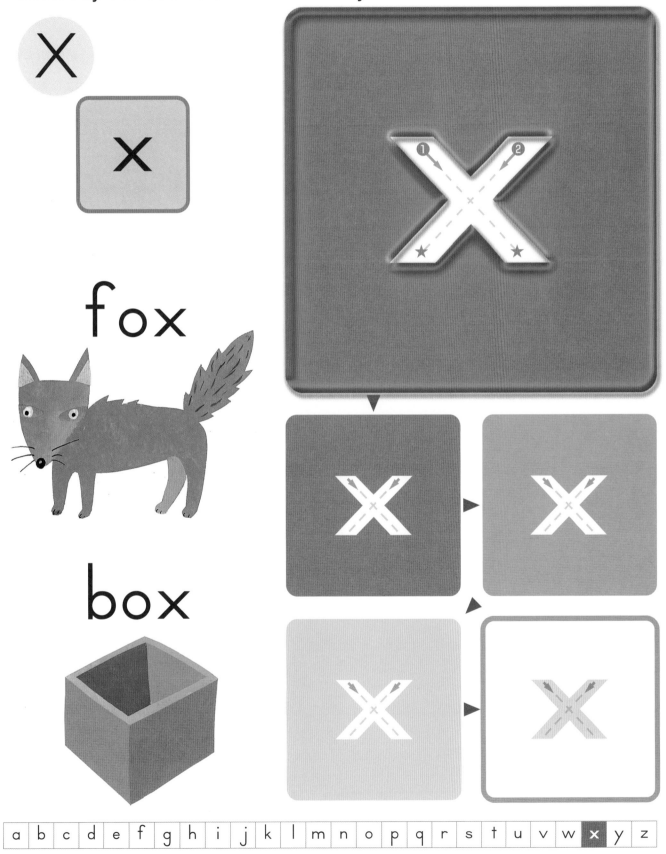

X

x

fox

box

a b c d e f g h i j k l m n o p q r s t u v w **x** y z

■ Read the words aloud.
  Then say the sound of the letter as you trace it.

fox

fox

fo

box

box

bo

six

six

si

ox

ox

o

Review

Writing h, m, and x

Name

Date

■ Read the words aloud.
  Then say the sound of the letter as you trace it.

hat

mat

fox

h

m

x

h

m

x

h

m

x

h

m

x

■ Read the words aloud.
  Then say the sound of the letter as you trace it.

hand

house

milk

moon

6

six

ox

Tracing Letters
Writing y

Name

Date

▪ Read the words aloud.
  Then say the sound of the letter as you trace it.

Y

y

yard

yellow

| a | b | c | d | e | f | g | h | i | j | k | l | m | n | o | p | q | r | s | t | u | v | w | x | y | z |

■ Read the words aloud.
  Then say the sound of the letter as you trace it.

yard

yard

yard

ard

yellow

yellow

yellow

ellow

yell

yell

yell

ell

yo-yo

yo-yo

yo-yo

o-yo

18 Tracing Letters
Writing z

■ Read the words aloud.
Then say the sound of the letter as you trace it.

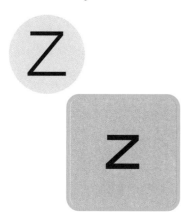

zebra

zipper

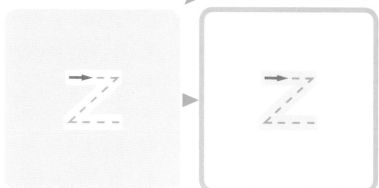

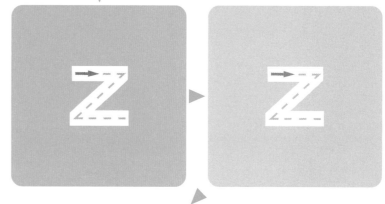

| a | b | c | d | e | f | g | h | i | j | k | l | m | n | o | p | q | r | s | t | u | v | w | x | y | z |

■ Read the words aloud.
  Then say the sound of the letter as you trace it.

zebra

zipper

zebra

zipper

ebra

ipper

zoo

zigzag

zoo

zigzag

oo

igzag

Name

Date

■ Read the words aloud.
Then say the sound of the letter as you trace it.

K

k

key

king

a b c d e f g h i j **k** l m n o p q r s t u v w x y z

■ Read the words aloud.
  Then say the sound of the letter as you trace it.

key

key

ey

king

king

ing

kick

kick

ick

kettle

kettle

ettle

Review
Writing y, z, and k

Name

Date

■ Read the words aloud.
Then say the sound of the letter as you trace it.

yard   zebra   key

y   z   k

y   z   k

y   z   k

y   z   k

■ Read the words aloud.
  Then say the sound of the letter as you trace it.

yell

yo-yo

zoo

zigzag

kick

kettle

Tracing Letters
Writing s

Name

Date

■ Read the words aloud.
Then say the sound of the letter as you trace it.

S

s

sun

sand

| a | b | c | d | e | f | g | h | i | j | k | l | m | n | o | p | q | r | s | t | u | v | w | x | y | z |

■ Read the words aloud.
  Then say the sound of the letter as you trace it.

sun

sun

sun

sand

sand

sand

snake

snake

snake

seven

seven

seven

Tracing Letters
Writing c

Name
Date

■ Read the words aloud.
  Then say the sound of the letter as you trace it.

C

c

cat

cup

a	b	c	d	e	f	g	h	i	j	k	l	m	n	o	p	q	r	s	t	u	v	w	x	y	z

■ Read the words aloud.
 Then say the sound of the letter as you trace it.

cat

cat

at

cup

cup

up

car

car

ar

cake

cake

ake

Tracing Letters
Writing o

■ Read the words aloud.
 Then say the sound of the letter as you trace it.

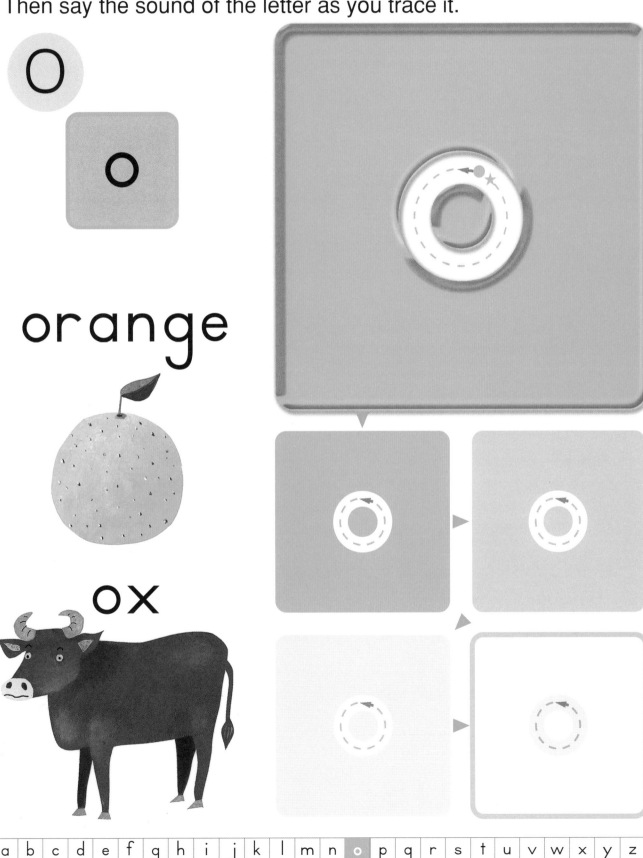

O

o

orange

ox

| a | b | c | d | e | f | g | h | i | j | k | l | m | n | o | p | q | r | s | t | u | v | w | x | y | z |

■ Read the words aloud.
   Then say the sound of the letter as you trace it.

orange

ox

orange

ox

orange

ox

octopus

ostrich

octopus

ostrich

ctopus

strich

Review

Writing s, c, and o

Name

Date

■ Read the words aloud.
Then say the sound of the letter as you trace it.

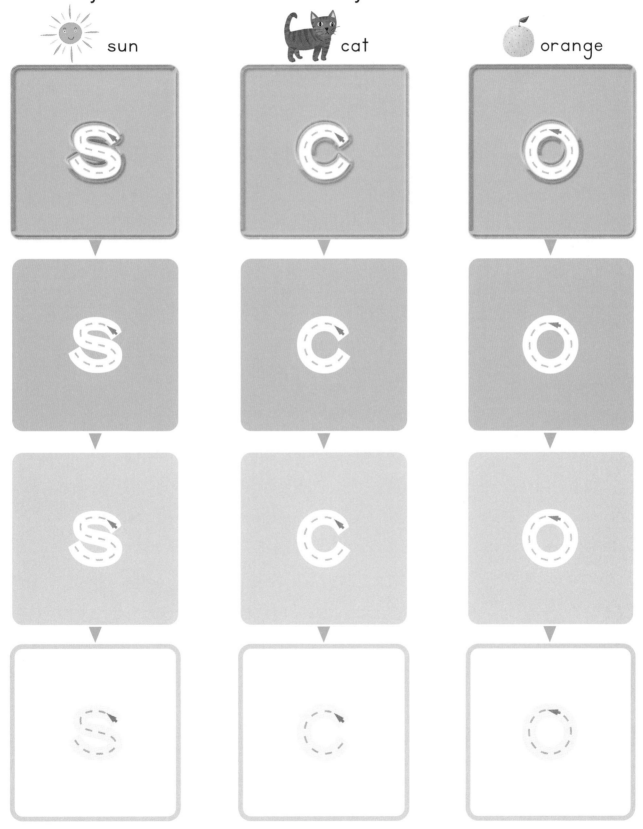

sun   cat   orange

■ Read the words aloud.
  Then say the sound of the letter as you trace it.

snake

seven

car

cake

octopus

ostrich

Name

Date

■ Read the words aloud.
Then say the sound of the letter as you trace it.

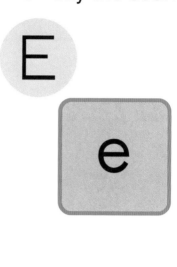

egg

elephant

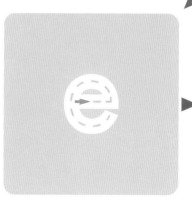

a b c d **e** f g h i j k l m n o p q r s t u v w x y z

■ Read the words aloud.
Then say the sound of the letter as you trace it.

egg

elephant

elbow

empty

Tracing Letters
Writing u

Name

Date

- Read the words aloud.
  Then say the sound of the letter as you trace it.

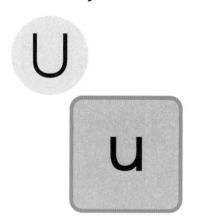

up

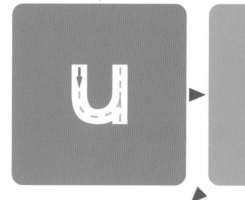

under

| a | b | c | d | e | f | g | h | i | j | k | l | m | n | o | p | q | r | s | t | u | v | w | x | y | z |

■ Read the words aloud.
  Then say the sound of the letter as you trace it.

up

up

up

under

under

under

uncle

uncle

uncle

umbrella

umbrella

umbrella

Tracing Letters
Writing a

Name

Date

- Read the words aloud.
  Then say the sound of the letter as you trace it.

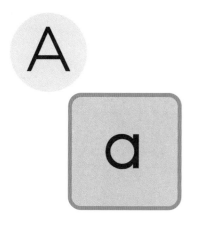

ant

apple

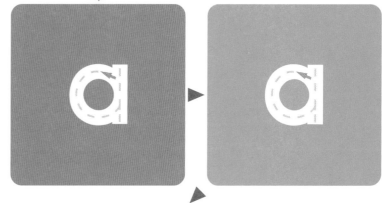

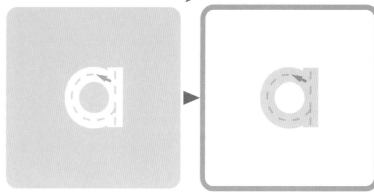

a b c d e f g h i j k l m n o p q r s t u v w x y z

- Read the words aloud.
  Then say the sound of the letter as you trace it.

ant

apple

ant

apple

nt

pple

ambulance

animals

ambulance

animals

mbulance

nimals

Name

Date

▪ Read the words aloud.
  Then say the sound of the letter as you trace it.

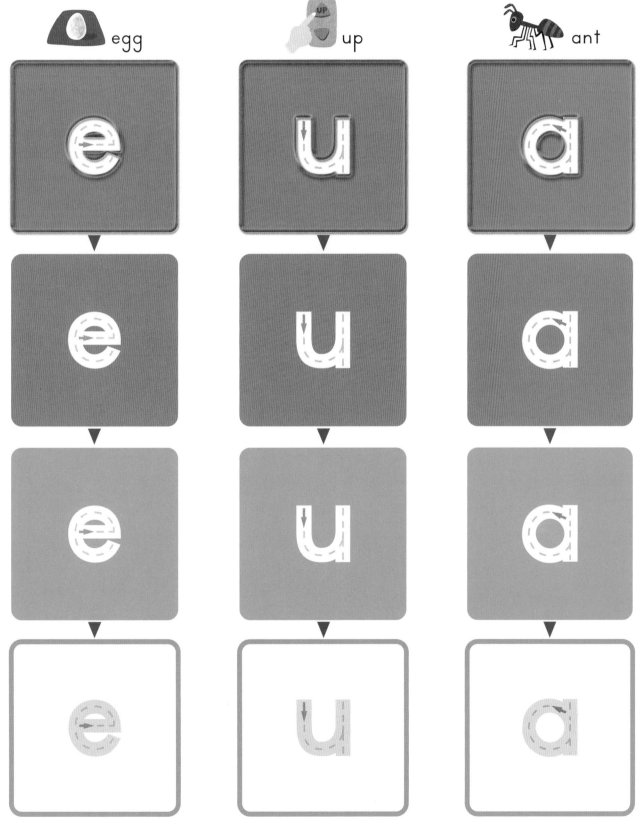

egg   up   ant

■ Read the words aloud.
  Then say the sound of the letter as you trace it.

elbow

empty

uncle

umbrella

ambulance

animals

Tracing Letters
Writing q

▪ Read the words aloud.
Then say the sound of the letter as you trace it.

Q

q

queen

quick

| a | b | c | d | e | f | g | h | i | j | k | l | m | n | o | p | q | r | s | t | u | v | w | x | y | z |

■ Read the words aloud.
  Then say the sound of the letter as you trace it.

queen

queen

queen

quick

quick

quick

quack

quack

quack

quilt

quilt

quilt

Name

Date

■ Read the words aloud.
  Then say the sound of the letter as you trace it.

G

g

gift

gum

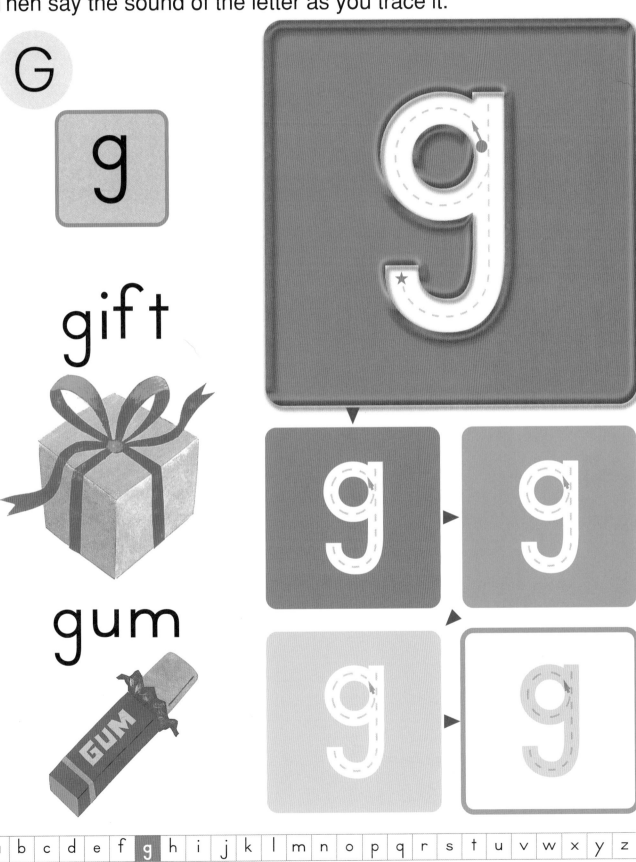

| a | b | c | d | e | f | g | h | i | j | k | l | m | n | o | p | q | r | s | t | u | v | w | x | y | z |

■ Read the words aloud.
  Then say the sound of the letter as you trace it.

gift

gift

gift

gum

gum

gum

girl

girl

girl

grass

grass

grass

Name	
Date	

■ Read the words aloud.
   Then say the sound of the letter as you trace it.

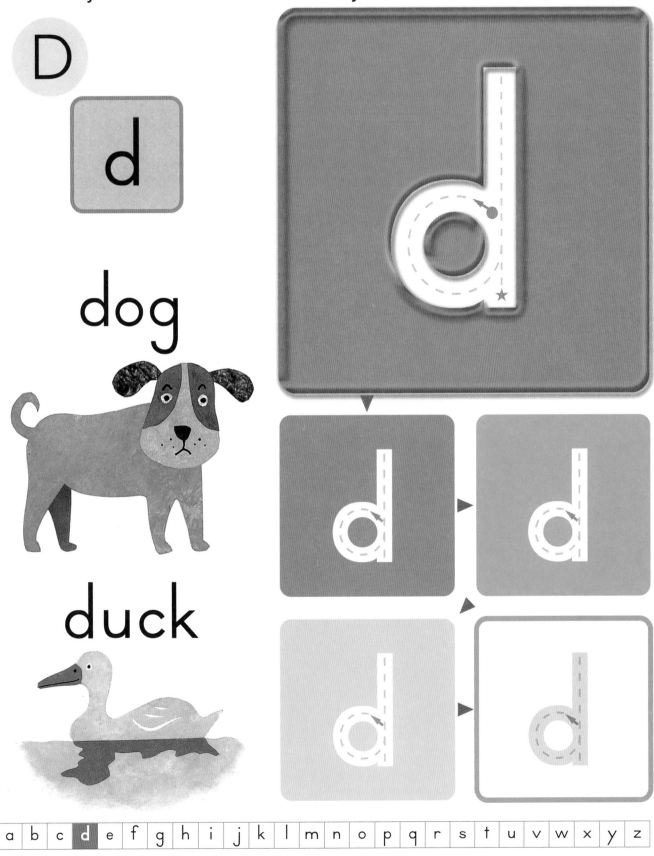

D

d

dog

duck

| a | b | c | **d** | e | f | g | h | i | j | k | l | m | n | o | p | q | r | s | t | u | v | w | x | y | z |

■ Read the words aloud.
  Then say the sound of the letter as you trace it.

dog

duck

dad

desk

Review

Writing q, g, and d

■ Read the words aloud.
Then say the sound of the letter as you trace it.

queen

gift

dog

q

g

d

q

g

d

q

g

d

q

g

d

■ Read the words aloud.
  Then say the sound of the letter as you trace it.

quack

quilt

girl

grass

dad

desk

Name

Date

- Read the words aloud.
  Then say the sound of the letter as you trace it.

B

b

bag

box

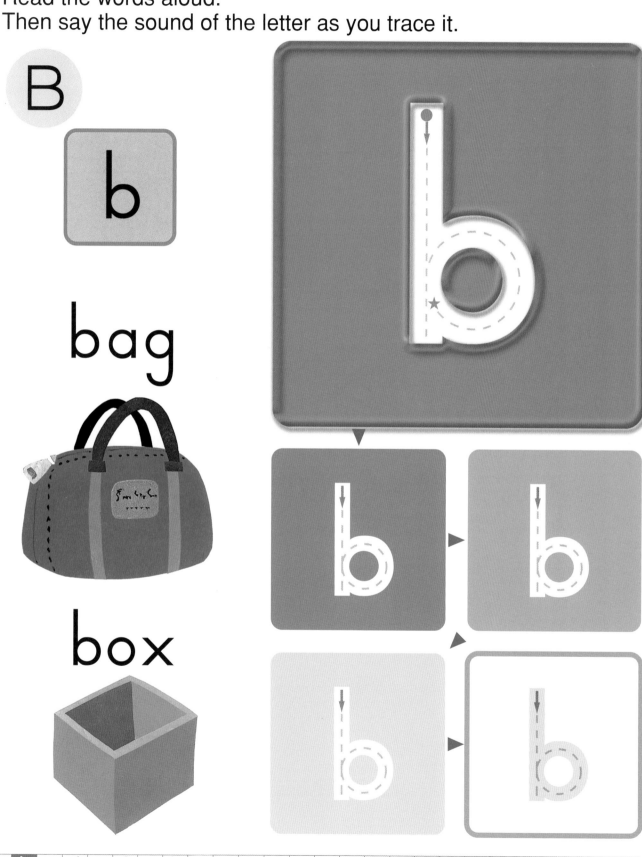

| a | **b** | c | d | e | f | g | h | i | j | k | l | m | n | o | p | q | r | s | t | u | v | w | x | y | z |

■ Read the words aloud.
  Then say the sound of the letter as you trace it.

bag

box

bed

bus

Tracing Letters
Writing p

Name

Date

■ Read the words aloud.
Then say the sound of the letter as you trace it.

P

p

pan

pig

| a | b | c | d | e | f | g | h | i | j | k | l | m | n | o | **p** | q | r | s | t | u | v | w | x | y | z |

■ Read the words aloud.
  Then say the sound of the letter as you trace it.

pan

pig

pencil

pants

Review
Writing b and p

▪ Read the words aloud.
  Then say the sound of the letter as you trace it.

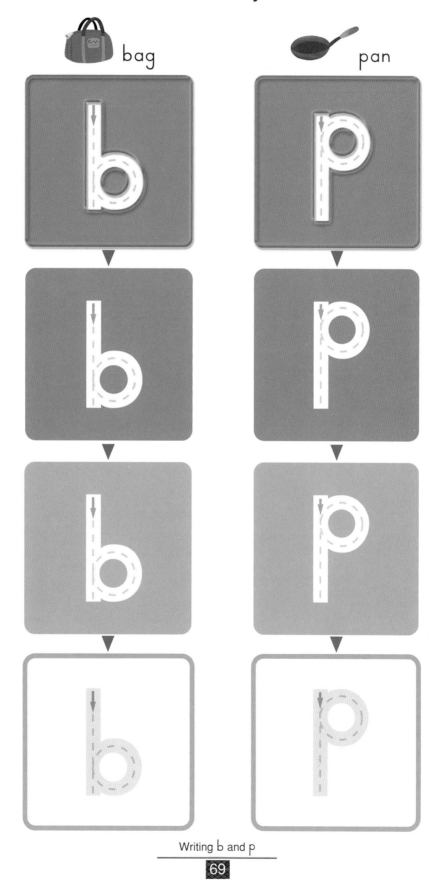

bag   pan

■ Read the words aloud.
 Then say the sound of the letter as you trace it.

bed

bus

pencil

pants

Name

Date

▪ Trace the letters a to i.

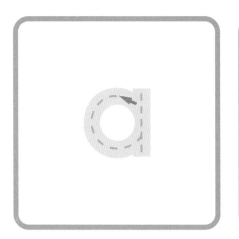

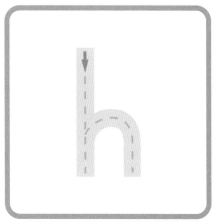

a b c d e f g h i j k l m n o p q r s t u v w x y z

■Trace the letters a to i.

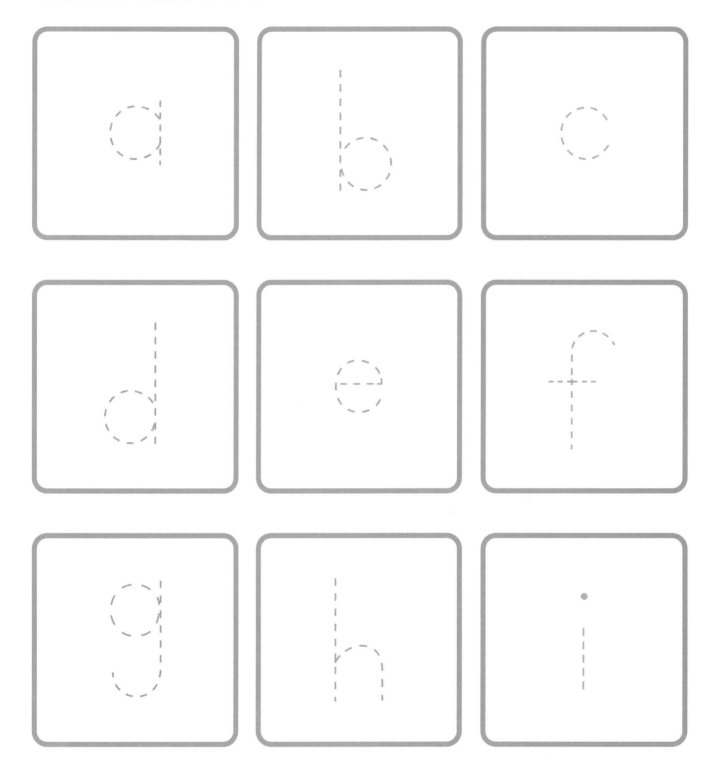

Name

Date

▪ Trace the letters j to r.

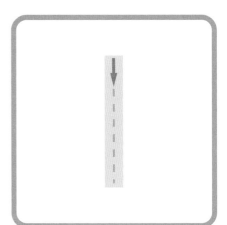

| a | b | c | d | e | f | g | h | i | j | k | l | m | n | o | p | q | r | s | t | u | v | w | x | y | z |

■Trace the letters j to r.

Review
Writing s-z

Name

Date

■ Trace the letters s to z.

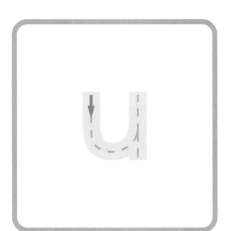

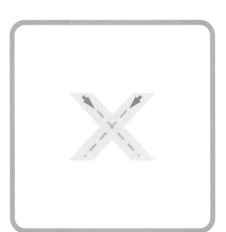

a b c d e f g h i j k l m n o p q r **s t u v w x y z**

■ Trace the letters s to z.

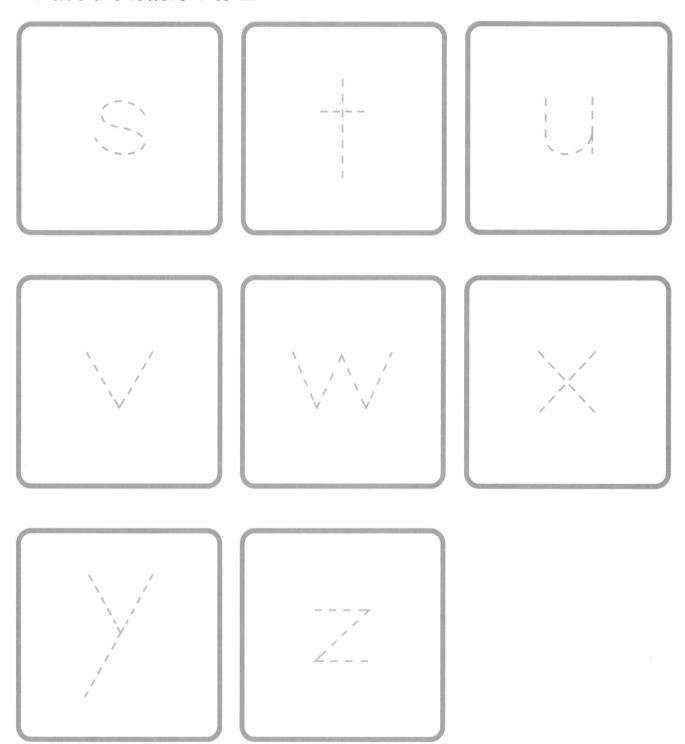

Review
Writing a-z

▪ Trace the letters a to z.

a

b

c

d

e

f

g

h

i

j

k

l

m

n

o

p

q

r

s

t

u

v

w

x

y

z

■ Trace the letters a to z.

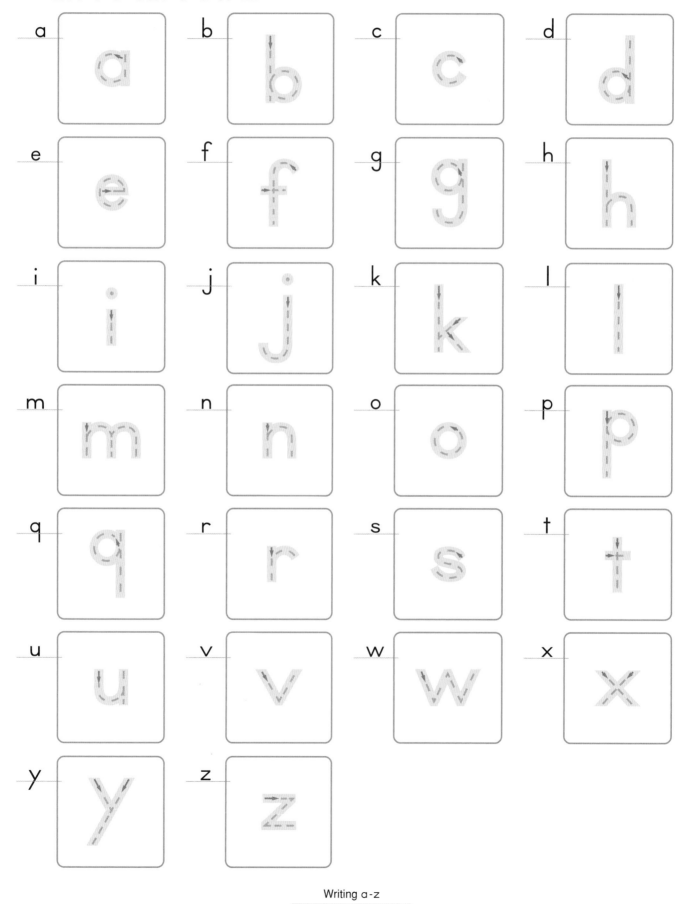

Review
Writing a-z

Name

Date

■ Trace the letters a to z.

a

b

c

d

e

f

g

h

i

j

k

l

m

n

o

p

q

r

s

t

u

v

w

x

y

z

■ Write the letters a to z, as shown on the left.

a

b

c

d

e

f

g

h

i

j

k

l

m

n

o

p

q

r

s

t

u

v

w

x

y

z

You are now able to read and write
lowercase letters a to z.
Congratulations!

Certificate of Achievement

_____

is hereby congratulated on completing

My First Book of Lowercase Letters

Presented on _____ , 20___

_____
Parent or Guardian